Moonlight Wonder

By Patricia Clark Smith

Illustrated By Amy L. A. Smith

Order this book online at www.trafford.com
or email orders@trafford.com

Most Trafford titles are also available at major online book retailers.

Print information available on the last page.

ISBN: 978-1-4907-8763-3 (sc)
ISBN: 978-1-4907-8762-6 (e)

Library of Congress Control Number: 2018935670

Because of the dynamic nature of the Internet, any web addresses or links contained in this book may have changed since publication and may no longer be valid. The views expressed in this work are solely those of the author and do not necessarily reflect the views of the publisher, and the publisher hereby disclaims any responsibility for them.

Our mission is to efficiently provide the world's finest, most comprehensive book publishing service, enabling every author to experience success. To find out how to publish your book, your way, and have it available worldwide, visit us online at www.trafford.com

Any people depicted in stock imagery provided by Getty Images are models, and such images are being used for illustrative purposes only.
Certain stock imagery © Getty Images.

Trafford rev. 02/23/2018

 www.trafford.com

North America & international
toll-free: 1 888 232 4444 (USA & Canada)
fax: 812 355 4082

Dedication

"Moonlight Wonder" is dedicated to my ancestors, relatives, family, and friends who have ever looked up at our ancient moon and wondered.

*****

"When the Celtic Imagination searched for the structures of shelter and meaning, it raised its eyes to the mountains and the heavens and put its trust in the faithful patterns of the sun, stars, moon and seasons…There they glimpsed a vision of order which was to become the heart of their understanding of beauty."
--John O'Donohue (2003)

Moonlight Wonder

Hello moonlight, you've traveled so far,
Your journey has ended; did you come from a star?

So quiet, so gentle, so peaceful, so soft,
You pour through my window from your home far aloft.

You've stories to tell of the places you've been,
You've knowledge to share from sights way back when.

The wisdom you've learned shouldn't end, as the dawn takes the place of the night, and our moment is gone.

4

The moonlight was silent; I stared from my chair,
I wondered and waited for a message somewhere.

I admired the cactus bathed in the moonlight,
I looked at the curtains, the moonlight made white.

I looked to the window the light came in through
And out up into the sky of dark blue.

There in the distance I stared at the moon,
For a moment or more an old friendship resumed.

"If the craters and stones on my surface could speak,
They'd ask the same question that you ask of me."

"The light on my surface is a traveling light,
A guest on a journey to make the world bright."

"This moonlight you graciously attribute to me,
Is the light of the evening, the light of the sea."

In school we have learned that scientists believe,
Big Bang theory explains everything that we see.

But, answers of scientists so far, far away,
Do not seem enough on this brand new fall day.

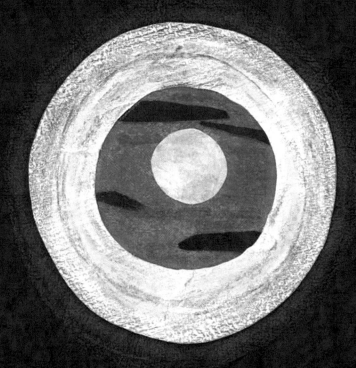

10

Maybe the question is not the beginning,
But the pattern of life this old light was bringing.

No beginning, no end as the morning dawn broke,
I looked to the sun for answers to stoke.

"The light that you see, that you think comes from me,
Is a sign of life's energy the world gives for free."

"The source of the moonlight you see on your floor,
Starts in the same place all good things start o're..."

"In the air, in the sky, in the water, in land,
And if you look closely, in the palm of your hand."

Yes! I realized to my own relief,
The heart is the center, the light of belief.

Within its small chambers, within old and young,
The answer's unfolding for the meaning of love.

The moonlight has taught me to look in my heart,
For knowledge and wisdom, there from the start.

And, maybe the theory scientists tell of,
Was really the "*Bang*" of the heart of just One,

Burst open with all the love that we need,
To live and to be as He meant us to be.

The moonlight which comes from the sun and the stars,
From galaxies and lands far, far away from ours,

Will warm my heart's light as the new day begins,
To carry the message, *the secret's within.*

Moon Garden

Moonlight spotlights tiny white daisies,
Daytime understudies of the summer garden,
Eclipsed by the red rose,
Upstaged by the tiger lily.

Patient little blossoms, contemplative buds,
Bathed in soft light,
Transcendent light,
Arise and dance for joy.

Midnight majesty above the dark shadows,
Simple white daisies,
Moonlight's masterpiece,
Image of Love.

(P.C.Smith – 1996)

Harvest Herald

Hope hangs high
In the evening sky,
Haloed, hallowed,
Harvest moon.

Peaceful usher,
Patient guide,
Shines pure light
Through the dark abyss.

Lunar majesty's transformation,
Celtic celebration,
Aesthetic joy,
Herald of hope.

(P.C.Smith – 1996)

Moon Maiden

Moon maiden
Celestial mother
Handmaid of
The night.

Simple, cratered,
Furrowed surface,
Mirror of
Eternal light.

Night time companion,
Midnight minister,
Comforter, guide,
Hope's delight.

(P.C.Smith – 1996)

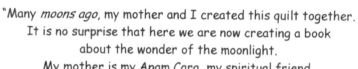

"Many *moons ago*, my mother and I created this quilt together.
It is no surprise that here we are now creating a book
about the wonder of the moonlight.
My mother is my Anam Cara, my spiritual friend,
and this book is our *heart-work...*"

--Amy Loretta Ann Smith - 2018

Printed in the United States
by Baker & Taylor Publisher Services